A gift for

....

From

....

Date

....

THE
WEEKLY
HABITS
PROJECT

A CHALLENGE TO JOURNAL, REFLECT, AND MAKE TINY CHANGES FOR BIG RESULTS

ZONDERVAN®

ZONDERVAN

The Weekly Habits Project

Copyright © 2023 by Zondervan

Requests for information should be addressed to:

Zondervan, 3900 Sparks Dr. SE, Grand Rapids, Michigan 49546

ISBN 978-0-310-46410-5 (HC)

Scripture quotations marked AMP are taken from the Amplified® Bible (AMP). Copyright © 2015 by The Lockman Foundation. Used by permission. www.lockman.org

Scripture quotations marked CEV are taken from the Contemporary English Version. Copyright © 1991, 1992, 1995 by American Bible Society. Used by permission.

Scripture quotations marked ESV are taken from the ESV® Bible (The Holy Bible, English Standard Version®). Copyright © 2001 by Crossway, a publishing ministry of Good News Publishers. Used by permission. All rights reserved.

Scripture quotations marked THE MESSAGE are taken from THE MESSAGE. Copyright © 1993, 2002, 2018 by Eugene H. Peterson. Used by permission of NavPress. All rights reserved. Represented by Tyndale House Publishers, Inc.

Scripture quotations marked NASB are taken from the New American Standard Bible® (NASB). Copyright © 1960, 1962, 1963, 1968, 1971, 1972, 1973, 1975, 1977, 1995 by The Lockman Foundation. Used by permission. www.lockman.org

Scripture quotations marked NIV are taken from the Holy Bible, New International Version®, NIV®. Copyright © 1973, 1978, 1984, 2011 by Biblica, Inc.® Used by permission of Zondervan. All rights reserved worldwide. www.Zondervan.com. The "NIV" and "New International Version" are trademarks registered in the United States Patent and Trademark Office by Biblica, Inc.®

Scripture quotations marked NLT are taken from the Holy Bible, New Living Translation. Copyright © 1996, 2004, 2015 by Tyndale House Foundation. Used by permission of Tyndale House Publishers, Inc., Carol Stream, Illinois 60188. All rights reserved.

Scripture quotations marked The Voice are taken from The Voice™. Copyright © 2012 by Ecclesia Bible Society. Used by permission. All rights reserved. Note: Italics in quotations from The Voice are used to "indicate words not directly tied to the dynamic translation of the original language" but that "bring out the nuance of the original, assist in completing ideas, and . . . provide readers with information that would have been obvious to the original audience" (The Voice, preface).

Any internet addresses (websites, blogs, etc.) and telephone numbers in this book are offered as a resource. They are not intended in any way to be or imply an endorsement by Zondervan, nor does Zondervan vouch for the content of these sites and numbers for the life of this book.

Art direction and cover design: Tiffany Forrester

Cover and interior photo credit: Noelle Glaze

Interior design: Kristy Edwards

Printed in India

23 24 25 26 27 28 29 30 31 32 33 /REP/ 15 14 13 12 11 10 9 8 7 6 5 4 3 2 1

THE
WEEKLY
HABITS
PROJECT

Contents

Our Hands

Our Everything

Introduction

How to Use This Journal

*"Remember not the former things, nor
consider the things of old. Behold, I am
doing a new thing; now it springs forth, do
you not perceive it? I will make a way in
the wilderness and rivers in the desert."*

ISAIAH 43:18–19 ESV

Aspiring to start a new habit or stop a bad one is a
universally human experience. It's easy to get swept up in
the promise of newness. But like a sparkler, our motivation can
quickly fizzle out. Many times we press on only as far as sheer
will and self-denial can carry us.

Too often, the habits we aspire to are rooted in
comparison. We try to emulate those around us who seem to
have the good life figured out. Other times, our aspirations
are crowded out by distraction; rather than creating space for
discipline, we try to cram in one more thing.

But here's the good news: God is inviting you to something
bigger and more fulfilling, an experience that springs forth
renewal and refreshment. He wants to do a new thing in you.
Maybe you have a sense of what that is, or maybe you need
help finding it. Maybe it's a complete overhaul, or maybe
it's just a tiny step forward. Use this journal to connect with
Scripture and reflect on what God wants to make new in your
life through your thoughts, feelings, and actions as you move
toward meaningful change.

Our
Minds

Giving Our Thoughts to God

*"Remember not the former things,
nor consider the things of old."*

ISAIAH 43:18 ESV

How you think about yourself and your situation can empower you with possibility—or it can make you a victim to destructive patterns. If we're not careful, we can find ourselves locked up in our past, which robs us of the good things God is giving us in the present. We might fixate on what we need to let go of, hold on too tightly to our mistakes, or trap ourselves in old identities.

These limiting beliefs can get in the way of God's plan for you. The prophet Isaiah reminds us that the same God who delivered His people is doing a new thing in our midst. It's easy to read the Old Testament and wonder why the Israelites had a hard time believing God's promise to give them hope and a future in a promised land. After decades of walking in the desert, we can see why they might have grumbled and complained. But are we any different? Do we trust that God can help us change and work things together for our good?

WEEK 1

Strive for Better

*"Instead, seek his kingdom, and these
things will be added to you."*

LUKE 12:31 ESV

What does it mean to strive after God's kingdom? It's an invitation to a different way of living, an alternative to the world's way. When we make the effort to know God and the way of His kingdom, the minutiae and concerns of everyday life fade. His bigger purpose comes into focus.

Jesus asks us to notice the habits and rhythms of the natural world as a way of living. In His famous Sermon on the Mount, He points out our habit of worry, born from a fear that says there will not be enough. But then Jesus asks us to consider how the ravens and the fields of lilies live. They don't have an awareness of scarcity—they simply live and grow by moving through the natural rhythms of each day.

The kingdom Jesus invites us into is a new way of living, steeped in humility and trust. So root yourself in what you know about God and His kingdom. From there, your trust in God will grow.

What creates worry or anxiety in your life? Name these things and give them to God.

....

....

....

....

Have your worries become a habit? What fears are they tied to?

....

....

....

....

Take a moment to meditate on the abundance of nature and what it reveals about God.

....

....

....

....

....

Listen and Lean In

*Focus on what you are doing as you go to the
house of God and draw near to listen. . . . Do
not be hasty with your mouth or impulsive
in thought to bring up a matter before
God. For God is in heaven and you are on
earth; therefore let your words be few.*

ECCLESIASTES 5:1–2 AMP

I s it any surprise that amid the noise of a busy world, God
is calling you to be quiet? It's hard enough to find a quiet
space, but it's even harder to quiet your mind. Use the prompts
in these verses to slow down, step off the mental fast track, and
spend some time with God.

Know that God hears you, both what is spoken and
unspoken. Before you pick up the conversation and start
talking to Him again, set aside time to listen first. It may bring
clarity to your struggle as you dial into a heavenly perspective.

As you come into God's presence, focus on what
you are doing. What distractions do you need to put
aside?

....

....

....

....

....

....

How does it feel to be in His house? Acknowledge that He is God in heaven, and you are on Earth.

....

....

....

....

....

....

Draw near to listen: What does God have for you in this moment? If it's just the quiet, accept this gift.

....

....

....

....

....

Keep in Step

*For everything the flesh desires goes against
the Spirit, and everything the Spirit desires
goes against the flesh. There is a constant
battle raging between them that prevents
you from doing the good you want to do.*

GALATIANS 5:17 The Voice

Whenever you set a new habit in motion, it doesn't take long to feel the struggle setting in too. But God has given you a gift for moments like this: His Spirit. So which fruit of the Spirit do you need more of right now? Love, joy, peace, patience, kindness, goodness, faithfulness, gentleness, or self-control (Galatians 5:22–23)?

Turn your attention from what's holding you back, and instead focus on God's promise. You'll not only find what it takes to overcome your struggles; you'll know the freedom and fullness that come from life with God.

When you're establishing new habits, what's your biggest struggle?

....

....

....

....

....

....

....

....

 Which fruits of the Spirit would help you most? For example, if finding time is hard, you might pray for more self-control and peace.

....

....

....

....

....

....

....

....

....

....

Move from Knowing to Doing

"Who then is the faithful and wise manager, whom his master will set over his household, to give them their portion of food at the proper time? Blessed is that servant whom his master will find so doing when he comes."

LUKE 12:42–43 ESV

Being a faithful and wise manager requires both knowing *and doing*. In this parable, Jesus holds up the manager's willingness to care for people and consistently carry out the rhythms of everyday life to show us how to live. Our ambition to do important things can lead us to believe that we are not ready to act. In this passage Jesus conveys the urgency of carrying out the daily actions God has entrusted to us. Don't make the task at hand so big or important that you can't complete it. Let what you know about God and the ways of His kingdom inform how you conduct your day and how you treat others.

Which is easier for you: knowing or doing? How do you stall or delay what you need to do?

....

....

....

....

....

....

....

Think about your ambition. Does it line up with God's kingdom way of living? Why or why not?

....

....

....

....

....

....

....

....

Ask for Discernment

*Give your servant therefore an understanding
mind to govern your people, that I may
discern between good and evil, for who is
able to govern this your great people?*

1 KINGS 3:9 ESV

God appeared to Solomon in a dream, and even in that altered state, he had the clarity to ask God for discernment. This pleased God so much that He granted Solomon wisdom and understanding, *and* He gave him "breadth of mind like the sand on the seashore" (1 Kings 4:29 ESV). It's hard to fathom this kind of abundance, but let's take a look at what preceded it.

When we study the patterns of Solomon's life, we see that he put God first. He loved God, he strived to live according to God's statutes, and he brought his offerings before God. Solomon recognized God's role in making him king, and he was aware of his own shortcomings.

Discernment feels lofty, but Scripture shows that it's the ability to know good from evil, light from dark. When the patterns of your life reflect your love for God and willingness to serve Him, discernment becomes easier—because you're closer to the Source of all wisdom.

Solomon's request empowered his kingdom because it equipped him to serve God and live out his purpose.

How do the patterns of your life reflect your love for God? Do you regularly go to Him for wisdom?

....

....

....

....

....

....

Are you in need of discernment, to know good from evil, light from dark? Bring your request to the Source of wisdom.

....

....

....

....

....

....

....

....

The Point of Purpose

*The purpose in a man's heart is like deep water,
but a man of understanding will draw it out.*

PROVERBS 20:5 ESV

God has a purpose for you—that is a promise you can cling to. You might not think of pursuing your purpose as a habit to work on, but because it can be such a difficult and lofty pursuit, it's worth coming back to regularly.

Purpose is like the deep water described in the verse above. If you've ever spent time trying to find something at the bottom of deep water, you know how murky it is. It can feel the same way when you're trying to unpack your purpose—it's not always clear or immediate.

Even if you have a sense of your purpose, your life plan can suddenly change. And just like that, you're back in the dark, deep water, trying to search for it again.

Here's a daily rhythm to help you through all that is unknowable: Go to the Source and draw out the water. Keep doing this every day, and eventually, your purpose will play out.

How do you respond to the parts of life that you can't control or know?

....

....

....

....

....

....

....

 Reflect on a time when you felt God's purpose playing out in your life. Are there patterns from that time that would benefit you now?

....

....

....

....

....

....

....

....

Dial Down Distraction

*For the time will come when they will not
tolerate sound doctrine; but wanting to have
their ears tickled, they will accumulate for
themselves teachers in accordance with their
own desires, and they will turn their ears away
from the truth. . . . But as for you, use self-
restraint in all things, endure hardship, do the
work of an evangelist, fulfill your ministry.*

2 TIMOTHY 4:3–5 NASB

What is it that tickles your attention, feeds your desires, and entices you to keep coming back for more? We regularly get bombarded with opinions and images and content—and it's not all sound or good for our souls. Technology puts all of it at our fingertips, feeding our appetite for distraction or offering straight-up avoidance. And the more we take in, the harder it becomes to walk in truth.

The life God has for you will require you to engage with the world, but you can do so with intention. What does that look like? Inviting God into your own brokenness and helping others experience His love in the process. To do this well and to fulfill your ministry, be aware of the habits that creep into your daily life and compromise your ability to walk in God's life-giving truth.

What distracts you from spending more time with God?

What is one small action you can take to rein in your relationship with technology?

How can you engage with the world intentionally while seeking God's truth?

Choose to Be Known

*God, investigate my life; get all the facts
firsthand. I'm an open book to you; even from
a distance, you know what I'm thinking.*

PSALM 139:1–2 MSG

As important as it is for people to feel seen and heard, how much better is it to be known? When we're fully known, there's an implied unconditional acceptance, whatever our flaws, whatever the story that's unfolding in our lives.

As you train your mind on the things God cares most about, you'll need to practice discernment and discipline. And you will undoubtedly battle distraction. But every step of the way, you will be known by God . . . and loved unconditionally. Your willingness to be known by God matters. Invite Him to investigate your life. Make yourself an open book. Take inventory of any nooks and crannies where it feels as if God is removed, cut off, or less relevant.

What stands in the way of you feeling known by God? What areas have you closed off to Him?

....
....
....
....
....
....
....

Ask God to investigate your life this week. Can you make yourself an open book to Him each day?

....
....
....
....
....
....
....

Engage Doubt

Immediately the boy's father cried out and said, "I do believe; help my unbelief!"

MARK 9:24 NASB

We have all felt doubt. It comes in many shapes and sizes. There's the stubborn kind where you don't want to be wrong, so you dig in. There's the quiet kind you don't talk about, but you can hear it whisper in the stillness. And there's the doubt born of long periods of struggle and suffering.

In this encounter with Jesus, a father was desperate for his son to be healed. His son was controlled by demons, and every effort the father had made up to this point had fallen short. When he heard that belief would bring healing, the father mustered all the belief he had left and asked Jesus to help him with the doubt that remained.

In this dire situation, the father chose to engage his doubt in exchange for the sheer potential of something better. It's undeniable: engaging doubt creates space for hope.

How does doubt show up in your life? Is it a lack of
trust in God, self-doubt, or something else?

....

....

....

....

....

....

How can you engage with doubt this week? Breathe
deeply and ask God to restore your hope.

....

....

....

....

....

....

....

Make Room for Iteration

So then, my beloved, just as you have always
obeyed, not as in my presence only, but now
much more in my absence, work out your
own salvation with fear and trembling.

PHILIPPIANS 2:12 NASB

What does it look like to "work out your own salvation"? Even though it's all-important work, in this verse, Paul was talking to his closest friends about the everyday effort to follow God. It can be hard, right? Because each day brings its own challenges, and what worked yesterday might not be effective today.

Cue the fear and trembling—working out your salvation is not for the faint of heart! But read on to verse 13, and you can take hope in the fact that you are not alone. God Himself is at work in you.

Each day is a chance for a new iteration of faith. Imagine that you are a jazz player, and it's up to you to pick up the tune in a way that responds to the challenges of the day. The rhythm will carry you, but the melody will look a little different. And that is okay.

How will you work out your salvation through your daily habits this week? Where is God at work?

....
....
....
....
....
....

How can you make room for things to look different than you have planned?

....
....
....
....
....
....
....
....
....

Process, Not Perfection

*I am sure of this, that he who began
a good work in you will bring it to
completion at the day of Jesus Christ.*

PHILIPPIANS 1:6 ESV

As we try to train our minds on the will of God, this verse is a good reminder of what matters most. The promise is *completion*, not *perfection*. What a relief! Not only is it acceptable to *not* be perfect . . . there is a finish line, and you will reach it.

How often do you find yourself striving after perfection or focusing on your mistakes? The real problem with our perfection obsession is that it puts the focus on us, not God. It's a subtle thing, but the simple effort to emulate Jesus is likely to be more effective than the hard work we might put in to solve a problem or polish up our best efforts.

| How are you a work in progress?

....

....

....

....

....
....
....
....
....

 Take a moment to think about how God sees you now. How does this differ from how you see yourself?

....
....
....
....
....
....
....
....
....
....
....
....

Reframe Mistakes

"This is what the LORD says: 'When people fall down, don't they get up again? When they discover they're on the wrong road, don't they turn back?'"

JEREMIAH 8:4 NLT

Falling down spiritually is a fact of life. Your day fills up, and you don't set aside time to meet with God. You make a decision that seems of little consequence, and three choices later, you can see that you're headed in the wrong direction.

Notice that God doesn't say *if* you will fall down; He knows it will happen. Spend time with the Old Testament minor prophets, and you'll understand how far God will go to encourage us to get back up, to turn around, and to start again.

You are on a journey. Along the way you might stumble, grumble, or wander. What are you learning in these moments? Use these lessons to reorient yourself.

Reflect on some of the mistakes you've made this year. Did consistency play a part?

....

....

....

....

....

....

 What do you need to start again? How can you be more consistent this time around?

....

....

....

....

....

....

....

....

....

Knowing God Is Love

*Dear friends, let us continue to love one another,
for love comes from God. Anyone who loves is a
child of God and knows God. But anyone who
does not love does not know God, for God is love.*

1 JOHN 4:7–8 NLT

We typically think of our head and heart as a contrast between what's rational and what's emotional. At first glance, you would think they'd behave like oil and water: complete opposites of each other, always separate. But your heart and head work together much better than that.

Cultivating a habit takes discipline, which starts in your mind; it begins when you decide to take action over and over. The *why* of your habit is set by your heart. Without a *why*, your discipline might fizzle out.

In striving to know God, we learn how to love others, the head and the heart at their best. Maybe you'd like to make showing God's love more of a habit because your relationships are important to you. When you make that decision, you'll cultivate daily actions to grow more like Him. When you remember why you wanted to do that in the first place, you'll keep up the habit. And in time, your heart will become attuned to His.

How does knowing the character of God help you love others?

....
....
....
....
....
....
....

How can you build a habit of showing God's love in your relationships this week?

....
....
....
....
....
....
....
....
....

Our
Hearts

Giving Our Feelings to God

"See, I am doing a new thing! Now it springs up;
do you not perceive it? I am making a way in
the wilderness and streams in the wasteland."

ISAIAH 43:19 NIV

Feelings can make or break a habit. For better or worse, our emotions carry a great deal of influence over how we choose to act. When fear gets in the way, we become impulsive and reactive, losing sight of what God has for us. We trade in the rich, new thing He promised for a cheaper replica.

So how do we know this new thing is happening? We put our senses to work. We see and feel what God has set in motion.

The Father intimately knows your needs, and He will provide for them. Prepare your heart to experience the good He has for you.

Change Needs Roots

"But blessed are those who trust in the Lᴏʀᴅ and have made the Lᴏʀᴅ their hope and confidence. They are like trees planted along a riverbank, with roots that reach deep into the water. Such trees are not bothered by the heat or worried by long months of drought. Their leaves stay green, and they never stop producing fruit."

JEREMIAH 17:7–8 ɴʟᴛ

It's a fact: hard times are going to come. And when your resources begin to dry up, you'll need to connect to your life source. (Remember that stream God promised in the wasteland in Isaiah 43:19?)

Jeremiah reminds us that those who trust in God are blessed, like a tree with deep roots. But God wants more for you than mere survival. He wants to see you thrive, which can only happen when you tap into His life-giving goodness.

As you start to carry out your habits, check in with your heart. Remember, the fruits of the Spirit you'll produce as a result of your habit will not only yield actions like love and self-control; they'll also give you feelings of joy and peace. When our roots reach deep into God's love, the effort to change comes with more ease. As a result, more fruit follows.

What hardships are you experiencing in this season? Choose one to trust God with this week.

....

....

....

....

....

....

....

Have you been able to make small changes? Have you seen or felt the fruits of those changes?

....

....

....

....

....

....

....

....

....

What Chokes Out Change

"Still others, like seed sown among thorns, hear the word; but the worries of this life, the deceitfulness of wealth and the desires for other things come in and choke the word, making it unfruitful."

MARK 4:18–19 NIV

Fear is especially effective at thwarting change at the heart level. The slow creep of scarcity over wants and needs, the fretting over what you cannot know or control; it all seems so inconsequential in the moment. Yet your responses to fear will ultimately choke out the good things God has for you.

It's easy to think that more money will solve a problem, or a glass of wine will erase a miserable day. But Jesus reminds us that these patterns we can get stuck in can settle into our hearts like thorns, working against our growth, preventing us from feeling the fullness of His love.

First John 4:18 states plainly that there is no fear in perfect love. Be committed to looking after your heart, doing the work to root out fear and make more room for love.

How does fear interrupt your good intentions to change?

....

....

....

....

....

....

....

....

What intention can you set that is specific to one of your fears, something you want to start or stop?

....

....

....

....

....

....

....

....

Conditioning the Heart

*For the word of God is living and active and
full of power [making it operative, energizing,
and effective]. It is sharper than any two-edged
sword, penetrating as far as the division of the
soul and spirit [the completeness of a person],
and of both joints and marrow [the deepest
parts of our nature], exposing and judging the
very thoughts and intentions of the heart.*

HEBREWS 4:12 AMP

Every new year, people resolve to be healthier. Gym
memberships skyrocket along with the sales of athleisure
wear. A month or two later, ambition has faded, the gym
crowds have thinned out, and athleisure is just a style. We wait
for a more pressing call to action to pick up healthy habits . . .
or we wait for the next new year.

So it goes with an on-again, off-again relationship with the
Word. Even though we feel lost, overwhelmed, or burdened day
after day, our Bibles sit untouched.

To condition your heart, you need to spend time reading
the Bible. This week's verses reveal both the power of God's
Word and why you might shy away from it—because sometimes
confronting the truth hurts. But conditioning your heart this
way will give you energy, make you whole, and bring you into
alignment with God's heart.

Use this week to meditate on a Bible passage. Write it here and read it every day.

....

....

....

....

....

....

What is God saying to you in this passage? Listen for His voice.

....

....

....

....

....

....

....

....

....

....

A Mustard Seed

"The kingdom of heaven is like a mustard seed, which a man took and sowed in his field; and this is smaller than all other seeds, but when it is fully grown, it is larger than the garden plants and becomes a tree, so that the birds of the sky come and nest in its branches."

MATTHEW 13:31–32 NASB

Have you ever seen a patchwork of vibrant yellow alongside a country road or noticed mustard planted between the tidy rows of an orchard? Mustard is used as a cover crop because it protects water quality and improves the fertility of the soil. And in the mustard seed, we have a front-row seat to the heart of God.

Not only can mustard go from being a tiny seed to a tree, but it's also capable of putting down deep roots even in dry conditions. It chokes out weeds and fights off pests. It attracts birds and insects that work as pollinators, helping the mustard spread. The resulting rich soil helps the crops grow.

You play a pivotal role in God's kingdom. The faith you bring, however insignificant it may seem—even when it's as small as a mustard seed—can grow beyond your expectations, providing goodness and mercy to others around you.

God's kingdom work can start off tiny, like a mustard seed. How have you seen small seeds of faith grow into something bigger?

....

....

....

....

....

....

....

How might your faith be helping others grow?

....

....

....

....

....

....

....

....

....

Choose to Be Renewed

Create in me a clean heart, God, and
renew a steadfast spirit within me.

PSALM 51:10 NASB

As sinners, we're no strangers to guilt and shame. We must be willing to confess our mistakes to God, to do the work of change. But only God can bring about restoration.

The sin in our lives can cause tremendous personal turmoil. King David had to repent before God in the aftermath of his affair with Bathsheba. It's not hard to imagine the wave of thoughts and feelings that led to the series of choices that brought David to that moment. David asked God for a steadfast spirit—resolute and unchanging. He recognized his desperate need for God's help to manage his conflicting desires.

Asking for renewal is an everyday prayer for mistakes big and small. Recognize that as a Christ-follower, this is the ongoing work that will allow you to experience the fullness of God's grace and love.

Acknowledge your harsh words, bottled-up anger, wrongdoing, or "not doing" before God—and the Creator of the universe will transform your heart.

Bring your sin to God in this moment and ask Him to cleanse you.

....

....

....

....

....

 Throughout the week, meditate on the prayer you just wrote. As you do, try to notice your feelings about yourself and your experience of God.

....

....

....

....

....

....

....

....

....

A Flood of Feelings

You say, "I am allowed to do anything"—
but not everything is good for you. And even
though "I am allowed to do anything," I
must not become a slave to anything.

1 CORINTHIANS 6:12 NLT

We enjoy freedom in Christ, and that freedom can teeter toward entitlement and justification if we don't continually put it in check. How do you do that? Try to evaluate aspects of your lifestyle, as Paul was urging the Corinthians to do. But don't forget to look inward.

Our emotions, thoughts, and actions can easily fall into a chain reaction that is driven by our flesh, not God's Spirit. In other words, it's all too easy to become a slave to your feelings. This kind of life is a continual struggle and far from the freedom God wants for us.

Jesus gives us a different way to live. He practiced empathy and compassion. He felt grief, demonstrated righteous anger, and redefined love. He was both authentic and in control of how He responded to a situation. Don't give control of your life to your feelings. Make a choice to serve God instead.

What feelings cause you to make compromises? How do your feelings affect your thoughts and actions?

....

....

....

....

....

....

....

Ask God to help you rein in unhelpful emotions.

....

....

....

....

....

....

....

....

....

....

A Heart Perspective

*But the L*ORD *said to Samuel, "Don't judge
by his appearance or height, for I have
rejected him. The L*ORD *doesn't see things the
way you see them. People judge by outward
appearance, but the L*ORD *looks at the heart."*

1 SAMUEL 16:7 NLT

Imagine Jesse's seven sons standing shoulder to shoulder
in anticipation, from the oldest to the youngest. Which one
would be anointed the future king of Israel? Even the prophet
Samuel found himself swept up in preconceived ideas. A king
would be tall and strong, likely the oldest and most capable.

God judges by a different standard. He is constantly
subverting the ways of the world, and here He compelled
Samuel to send for the eighth son (the *actual* youngest son!)
to receive His blessing. David was diligently looking after his
family's sheep, not striving to be king. But God already knew
young David had a heart for Him.

It's only human to care about outward appearance or
achievement, but how's your heart? Invite God to use even the
smallest tasks of each day to transform your heart and prepare
you for what's ahead.

What attitude do you bring to the work you do each day? What is your heart perspective?

....

....

....

....

....

....

Who or what are you striving for? Ask God to look at your heart and turn it toward Him.

....

....

....

....

....

....

....

....

....

....

Peace from God

*"Peace I leave with you; my peace I
give to you. Not as the world gives do
I give to you. Let not your hearts be
troubled, neither let them be afraid."*

JOHN 14:27 ESV

When Jesus was about to leave the world behind, the disciples were undoubtedly fearful about what lay ahead. At first Jesus seemed to offer the customary Jewish goodbye, *shalom*, which is the Hebrew word for *peace* and means "complete or whole."

But Jesus quickly clarified that His peace was different from the world's interpretation. He announced the coming of the Holy Spirit (v. 26), an advocate and helper who would bring God's peace, the only kind to make us whole and complete—an incredible parting gift.

Jesus wants you to experience His peace. The circumstances of this life will bring trouble—Jesus acknowledged that truth. However, if you lean into His words, you can feel His shalom making your heart whole.

Is there an area of your life in need of restoration or peace?

....
....
....
....
....
....

How you feel doesn't have to be dictated by the world around you. Call upon the Holy Spirit to quiet your heart and remind you of God's promises.

....
....
....
....
....
....
....
....
....

Prayer Takes Practice

*The moment we get tired in the waiting,
God's Spirit is right alongside helping us
along. If we don't know how or what to
pray, it doesn't matter. He does our praying
in and for us, making prayer out of our
wordless sighs, our aching groans. He
knows us far better than we know ourselves
. . . and keeps us present before God.*

ROMANS 8:27 MSG

How many times have you begun to pray, and the clutter in your head caused your conversation with God to sound like mindless banter? The next time this happens, remind yourself that God knows your heart, and His Spirit is interceding for you according to God's will for your life. In other words, God's got you.

Humanity waits for the redemption of our earthly bodies while we hope for what's to come. The waiting becomes more urgent when we experience suffering or even the aches and pains of getting older. But don't forget: your life with God is happening now, and prayer is a chance to be in His presence. You don't have to wait to be with God. How comforting is that?

As you make time to pray this week, be mindful of the Holy Spirit praying alongside you, knowing God's will for your life. How does that feel?

....

....

....

....

....

....

Put your prayer in writing as a way of practicing intentional prayer.

....

....

....

....

....

....

....

....

The Discipline of Love

When we love others, we know we belong to the truth, and we feel at ease in the presence of God. But even if we don't feel at ease, God is greater than our feelings, and he knows everything. Dear friends, if we feel at ease in the presence of God, we will have the courage to come near him.

1 JOHN 3:19–21 CEV

Do you ever avoid God because your heart's not in a good place? You long to feel at ease, but it seems impossible from where you stand. Maybe stress over work or too many commitments has you locked up. Maybe you're angry at how someone is treating you, or a deep fatigue in your bones has left you numb.

When feelings get too intense, they have a way of keeping us from the presence of God. The discipline of loving others is one way out. Even small gestures can be incredibly loving, such as offering a friendly hello or holding open a door for a stranger. If you stick with it, what starts out as an act of obedience will soften your heart and bring you back to God.

What feelings prevent you from spending time with God?

What is something small you can do to love others this week?

Make Room for Lament

*Listen to my cry, for I am in desperate
need; rescue me from those who pursue
me, for they are too strong for me.*

PSALM 142:6 NIV

There is a rhythm at work in the book of Psalms that is easy to miss if you read them one at a time. This rhythm includes giving God thanks and praise *and* acknowledging the presence of pain.

The lament offers us a way to process pain and suffering, both in our lives and in the world around us. Our hearts need to lament, not only in private but also with others and on behalf of others. When we invite God into our brokenness, He brings healing, allowing us to see His love more clearly.

While laments can be intense and even uncomfortable, the psalmist recognized God's promises and character while suffering. In Psalm 142:5, David said, "You are my refuge, my portion in the land of the living" (NIV).

What pain in your own life do you need to acknowledge in prayer?

....

....

....

....

....

🌿 | Is there a situation outside of your own experience
that you might bring before God?

....

....

....

....

....

....

🌿 | Name a promise God has kept or something you
know to be true of Him.

....

....

....

....

....

....

Thanks and Praise

*It is good to give thanks to the LORD, to
sing praises to your name, O Most High; to
declare your steadfast love in the morning,
and your faithfulness by night.*

PSALM 92:1–2 ESV

When giving thanks to God becomes part of the rhythm of your day, it not only pleases God; it brings good things to you too. For starters, it shifts your attention. The events of your day become a little less urgent when you put your focus on almighty God and His kingdom.

What's more, we know a habit of gratitude offers a feel-good factor. When you specifically tell someone why you are grateful for them, it is likely to strengthen your relationship. It's no different with your faith. When you give praise to God, your heart and soul are satisfied by His love.

Throughout the psalms there is talk of singing praises to God, dancing with joy, and playing the tambourine—it sounds like a great time! Music draws the head, heart, and hands into worship, expanding our experience of God.

What are you thankful to God for? Acknowledge where you see His goodness in your life.

....

....

....

....

....

....

....

How can you make thanks and praise part of your daily routine?

....

....

....

....

....

....

....

Embrace Humility

*Have this attitude in yourselves which was
also in Christ Jesus, who, as He already existed
in the form of God, did not consider equality
with God something to be grasped, but emptied
Himself by taking the form of a bond-servant
and being born in the likeness of men. . . .
He humbled Himself by becoming obedient
to the point of death: death on a cross.*

PHILIPPIANS 2:5–8 NASB

Jesus' humility has always been hard for people to reconcile. When the Israelites asked God for a king, they wanted what other nations had: someone with power and influence. Everything about the way Jesus lived demonstrated that God's kingdom is not like the world we know. As a servant King riding on a donkey, Jesus gave us a sneak peak of God's upside-down kingdom.

The Bible instructs us to clothe ourselves in humility and consider others better than ourselves. God asks us to humble ourselves before Him. Humility is a heart thing. It is born out of love and serves a purpose. It points to God's love and His promise of redemption. Jesus is our ultimate example.

How do you feel about humility? Does it come easily to you?

....

....

....

....

....

....

Reflect on Jesus' ministry and consider a time when His humility stood out to you. How can you follow His example?

....

....

....

....

....

....

....

....

....

Finding Contentment

*Not that I am speaking of being in need, for
I have learned in whatever situation I am
to be content. I know how to be brought low,
and I know how to abound. In any and every
circumstance, I have learned the secret of facing
plenty and hunger, abundance and need.*

PHILIPPIANS 4:11–12 ESV

P aul is quick to acknowledge that he can live in all kinds of
difficult circumstances because God is his strength in all
situations. To find contentment, he had to fully surrender his
life to God.

Are you willing to trust God and the plan
He has for your life? It's likely to include
both abundance and scarcity, blessing and
struggle, a land of milk and honey and
also wilderness. When you are able to
experience contentment regardless of
your circumstances, your heart is in
step with God.

Contentment is an abiding, soulful
satisfaction. It sustains you for the journey
because it's no longer about you. It's about
God in you.

Reflect on how you have demonstrated a growing commitment to God.

....
....
....
....

In what areas of your life do you need more of God's strength?

....
....
....
....
....

Ask God to help you experience contentment.

....
....
....
....

Our Hands

Giving Our Actions to God

"Listen carefully, I am about to do a new thing.
Now it will spring forth;
Will you not be aware of it?
I will even put a road in the wilderness,
Rivers in the desert."

ISAIAH 43:19 AMP

God asks us to see what He is doing and then join Him on the road to wholeness, which may be different from our own ideas and priorities. Maybe you started this journey determined to improve your health, your spiritual disciplines, or your relationships—all worthwhile pursuits. But maybe you've found the road God has for you requires a number of small changes instead—tiny shifts in how you think, love, and act.

God promises He will make a way for us. Better yet, He promises to sustain us with rivers in the desert. Use this section as a checkpoint to reevaluate your direction and drive. Our habits, even the good ones, can be rooted in selfish ambition or in a desire to prove ourselves worthy.

As you think about where and how God wants you to act, be on the lookout for what He is doing and how He is inviting you to join Him. See the evidence of His goodness in your life as proof that you are right where He wants you to be.

Doing and Being

*For by grace you have been saved through faith;
and this is not of yourselves, it is the gift of
God; not a result of works, so that no one may
boast. For we are His workmanship, created in
Christ Jesus for good works, which God prepared
beforehand so that we would walk in them.*

EPHESIANS 2:8–10 NASB

There is a constant tension between doing and being. Chances are that you lean into one with more ease than the other. And that's how God made you. But whether you thrive in the being or in the doing, you need a balance of both.

God's grace is a gift. It's not something you can earn with good works. In fact, you are *among* His good works, created with a purpose that you are uniquely equipped to fulfill. And in order to start your journey toward that purpose, you need to spend time in His grace. You need to be with Him there.

God's plan for the doing asks you to walk with Him, with your head, heart, and hands fully engaged. You won't do it perfectly, even if you are a doer through and through. Use these moments to recognize your need for God.

Which is easier for you, doing or being? Why?

....

....

....

....

Take a long breath in, thinking about God's provision in this moment. What is He providing for you today?

....

....

....

....

....

Slowly exhale a long breath, considering what God would have you do today. What is He asking of you?

....

....

....

....

See the Need

*Do not withhold good from those to whom
it is due, when it is in your power to do it.*

PROVERBS 3:27 ESV

Who has God put in your path? What gifts has He given to you to meet the needs you encounter? We know God is the giver of every good and perfect gift. And His gifts help you share His lifesaving love with others.

When we take the time to meet someone's need, we have an opportunity to make His love known. Whether you fill a physical need or an emotional one, you honor God by recognizing the worthiness in another person.

Set aside your fear of scarcity. You serve a God of abundance. The good you can give others is a gift from God, and He will keep on providing you with what you need. Take joy in your God-given power to act, to serve those He loves.

 Acknowledge any fear you have around the spirit of giving.

....

....

 Consider the phrase "when it is in your power to do it." How can you be more attentive to what others need?

....

....

....

....

....

How can you trust God's timing in your own circumstances?

....

....

....

....

....

....

....

....

Wait on God

*But those who wait for the LORD [who
expect, look for, and hope in Him] will
gain new strength and renew their power;
they will lift up their wings [and rise up
close to God] like eagles [rising toward the
sun]; they will run and not become weary;
they will walk and not grow tired.*

ISAIAH 40:31 AMP

Don't bother doing things without God. Your age, your strength, even your sheer desire are of no consequence in comparison to the glory of God. Isaiah has us sit at the foot of God's throne and contemplate the size and scope of His power. And for good reason! God's immeasurable glory and power changes what we see as possible.

You can be confident in the waiting, expectant that God's plan will be fulfilled—maybe even without you knowing it. So actively put your hope in Him. When it comes time to act, feel God's strength taking control. If you are tired, He will be your strength. If you have no influence by the world's standards, He will give you power (v. 29).

In what ways do you find yourself waiting on God? How is that going?

....

....

....

....

 Recall a time when you didn't wait on God's timing. How did that limit you?

....

....

....

....

....

 Meditate on the enduring portrait of hope and action in this week's verse.

....

....

....

....

Walk in Faith

He has told you, O man, what is good;
and what does the Lord require of you
but to do justice, and to love kindness,
and to walk humbly with your God?

MICAH 6:8 ESV

The rules God gave to Micah show that faith changes how we are to think, talk, and act. But these rules don't just apply to our relationship with God. As people of faith, God calls us to demonstrate His justice, kindness, and humility to others in how we live.

It's not enough to simply live with humility. We are meant to be in relationship with others. Perhaps we'd like to think that only kindness is the answer—not so. There are times when we need to right a wrong. And justice without kindness and humility is not God's way of doing things.

Admittedly, Micah's vision for a New Jerusalem marked by justice, kindness, and humility seemed highly unlikely to a divided nation wandering away from God. But from past to present, God is steadfast in His promise of restoration. We won't always get it right, but as believers we can align our thinking, talking, and doing in the direction of God's kingdom.

Do any of the habits you're working on involve justice, kindness, or humility? Which of these words give you pause, and why?

....
....
....
....
....
....

Rewrite this week's verse and incorporate it into a daily prayer, asking God to show you what He means by it.

....
....
....
....
....
....
....
....
....

Be All In

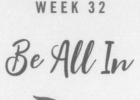

*"Hear, O Israel! The LORD is our God, the
LORD is the one [the only God]! You shall
love the LORD your God with all your heart
and mind and with all your soul and with
all your strength [your entire being]."*

DEUTERONOMY 6:4–5 AMP

It's difficult to sync your faith with the rest of a full life. The demands of family and friends, work, personal goals, and growth all seem to be in competition. God desires to be your one and only, over all of it.

Let's be real—loving God with all you are is not easy. God's people are asked to teach these words, repeat them daily, wear them on their bodies, post them in their homes, and write them on their hearts and minds. Some of your actions might look more like obedience, and that's okay! It's also the reason for all the reminders—repetition works.

Start each day by affirming your commitment to God. Commit to loving Him more fully and—over the long arc of your story—your mind, your emotions, and the very essence of who He made you to be will begin to work in a synchronized way more often.

Is there a particular segment of your life that feels out of sync?

....
....
....
....
....

 What small change can you consistently make in the week ahead to be obedient to God in this area?

....
....
....
....

 Where do you need reminders of God as your one and only?

....
....
....
....

Run the Race

*Since we stand surrounded by all those
who have gone before, an enormous
cloud of witnesses, let us drop every extra
weight, every sin that clings to us and
slackens our pace, and let us run with
endurance the long race set before us.*

HEBREWS 12:1 The voice

There is a handful of sports where individuals compete for the podium, but each competitor is scored as a team—cycling, cross-country running, track and field. It's easy to focus on the individual and lose the bigger picture.

We tend to do the same thing in our faith. We focus on our own race, our pursuit of God, forgetting that we run this portion of the race on the heels of Jesus followers who came before us, and at some point, we will hand off to those who come after us.

The "enormous cloud of witnesses" should inspire our striving. God is worthy of our individual efforts, but when we see our fellow believers live out God's calling, or think of the heroes of the faith, we are better equipped to run. Always remember: you aren't running alone. We run together.

How can you take encouragement from the heroes of the faith in Hebrews 11? What struggles or hardships are familiar to you?

....

....

....

....

....

 To run well you need to fix your eyes on Jesus (Hebrews 12:2). What can you do to limit distraction or deviation in the week ahead?

....

....

....

....

....

....

....

....

....

Lift Up Others

> *Whenever Moses held up his hand, Israel prevailed, and whenever he lowered his hand, Amalek prevailed. But Moses' hands grew weary, so they took a stone and put it under him, and he sat on it, while Aaron and Hur held up his hands, one on one side, and the other on the other side. So his hands were steady until the going down of the sun.*

EXODUS 17:11–12 ESV

This is a powerful image, Aaron and Hur holding up Moses' hands so that Joshua's army could defeat the opponent. God's plan somehow always grows to pull more people into it.

How might this play out in your life? Are you facing challenges where you need to call upon the strength of others? This can be difficult for some of us to do. We move through life like a maverick, doing things our own way and taking pride in our accomplishments.

In what circumstances do you need to come alongside someone else and be a support? As the dust settled on the battlefield, Aaron and Hur had a front-row seat to the power of God. You might walk away from lifting up others with more confidence in God and in what He can do.

How can you enlist others to help you with the particular areas of growth you're seeking?

....

....

....

....

....

....

....

Who can you commit to support in their growth or through an ongoing struggle? Pray for them here.

....

....

....

....

....

....

....

....

....

Rewards and Reversals

"And not only you, but anyone who sacrifices home, family, fields—whatever—because of me will get it all back a hundred times over, not to mention the considerable bonus of eternal life. This is the Great Reversal: many of the first ending up last, and the last first."

MATTHEW 19:29–30 MSG

God's kingdom is so starkly different from our experience of the world. Jesus spent many sermons detailing this culture clash and inviting us to live differently. He invites us to redirect our time, talent, and treasure to grow His kingdom.

However worthy God's work is, maybe you need this reminder to keep pressing on. Know that God sees how you have rearranged your week to help others. He sees you using your unique gifts to grow His church. He sees your generosity.

As for the rewards, God promises to reverse injustices. He'll make the last, the unseen, and the vulnerable first. He will also reverse the power of sin and death, opening the door to eternal life with Him.

Sit with these "Great Reversals" for a moment. How do you imagine God's kingdom and eternal life?

....
....
....
....
....

Are there any opportunities this week to sacrifice for the kingdom or to put yourself last?

....
....
....
....

How can you make a habit out of sacrifice?

....
....
....
....

Ruts and Grooves

"I know your deeds, that you are neither cold (invigorating, refreshing) nor hot (healing, therapeutic); I wish that you were cold or hot."

REVELATION 3:15 AMP

When things are going smoothly, it can be difficult to know whether you are in a groove or a rut. Complacency has a way of moving in so slowly that you don't notice. It can start with self-sufficiency. When you have the resources to address the problems that come up, you can be lulled into thinking that you have less need for God. A complacent attitude can also be triggered by pride—maybe serving others has somehow become all about you, or you ascribe to the mindset that "you know best."

When you're in a groove with God, you enjoy a steady flow of His life-giving water and pass it along to others. But when you allow your spiritual life, both the doing and being, to slip into autopilot, it affects how you show up in the world. Climb out of your rut and go back to the Source. God calls you out of complacency because He loves you. And He's made you for so much more.

Take your temperature—are you falling into complacency? If so, how are your spiritual habits reflecting this?

....
....
....
....

How much are you relying on God each day?

....
....
....
....

Do you need to make some adjustments to your daily routine so you can find your groove?

....
....
....
....

WEEK 37

Fighting Burnout

"The Spirit alone gives eternal life. Human effort accomplishes nothing. And the very words I have spoken to you are spirit and life."

JOHN 6:63 NLT

Burnout is a sure sign that you're acting on your own strength. You find yourself so invested in an outcome or goal that you sacrifice your physical and mental health as you strive to achieve it.

Jesus saw this coming, so He gave words for spirit and life. When you find yourself in these moments, you have a choice to make: submit to God and experience life with the Spirit . . . or strive and burn out repeatedly.

There is submission in following Christ—in the hard things, the complexity, and the waiting. Lean into the Spirit and let Him lead, and you will enjoy more ease as you live out your purpose.

In what ways are you experiencing burnout in this season?

....

....

....

....

....

....

....

What is it that you are reluctant to trust God with? Write a prayer committing it to God.

....

....

....

....

....

....

....

....

Being in Community

*Let us hold tightly without wavering to the hope
we affirm, for God can be trusted to keep his
promise. Let us think of ways to motivate one
another to acts of love and good works. And let
us not neglect our meeting together, as some
people do, but encourage one another, especially
now that the day of his return is drawing near.*

HEBREWS 10:23–25 NLT

People can complicate our experience of God. All of our flaws come out—we say things without thinking, we fail to understand another perspective, we jump to conclusions, we get offended. And yet God calls us to find community with others. He tells us that as believers, we make up one body with different parts for different purposes.

You are called to motivate and encourage others around you. This is how you help mobilize God's hope. Someone else will act and love differently than you, and that's a good thing.

Our differences can make us stronger if we hold on to God's promise. You will feel the same encouragement and motivation in community, and in you, others will see things they cannot do. Together we can do more and better demonstrate God's perfect love.

What frustrations do you experience in community?

....

....

....

....

How might some of the differences you see in others accomplish God's plan?

....

....

....

....

....

Write a prayer for God's wisdom as you navigate the complications of living in community.

....

....

....

....

Practicing Rest

*This is what the LORD says: "Stand at the
crossroads and look; ask for the ancient
paths, ask where the good way is, and walk
in it, and you will find rest for your souls.
But you said, 'We will not walk in it.'"*

JEREMIAH 6:16 NIV

The path God has for you provides rest. It's been part of His plan since the beginning of time, when He rested on the seventh day. God instructs us to prioritize rest each week. Rest makes space for satisfaction, and it helps you feel content with what you've accomplished.

What happens when you neglect rest? It's an all-too-familiar state—you find yourself running on empty, emotionally volatile or numb, and feeling alone.

God wants to give you rest and renewal for the journey. You might shake your head in disbelief at how God's people so often didn't listen and do what He asked of them, but this is our stubborn human will on display. Commit to habitual rest in each day, week, and season of your life.

How is your practice of rest going? How might you find more contentment and renewal in rest?

....

....

....

....

....

....

....

 Identify what keeps you from achieving rest on a regular basis. What can you give up or cut out to make more space for rest?

....

....

....

....

....

....

....

Serve Willingly

*Be shepherds of God's flock that is under your
care, watching over them—not because you
must, but because you are willing, as God wants
you to be; not pursuing dishonest gain, but
eager to serve; not lording it over those entrusted
to you, but being examples to the flock.*

1 PETER 5:2–3 NIV

As we serve God and others, there will be moments when it
feels more like work or an obligation. Maybe the joy fades
in the rush and stress of the week. Perhaps fewer people turn
out to help you serve. Or maybe you just aren't "feeling it."

God loves His people and is intentional about who
He trusts to take care of them—it's a privilege. When we
consistently show up, become part of the community, and set
an example in love, good things will happen. Blessings will
flow on all sides.

It's easy to look for growth and change as evidence that
what you're doing matters or that you're doing it well. It's only
human, but it's not God's way. Serving others with a spirit
of willingness plays a significant role in how God takes care
of you.

In what ways is it hard to bring a willing spirit to service? This can include friends and family.

....
....
....
....
....
....
....

 Think about how God sees the specific people He has entrusted to you. How might this change the way you show up for them?

....
....
....
....
....
....
....
....

WEEK 41

Work the Fallow Ground

*Sow for yourselves righteousness, reap
steadfast love; break up your fallow ground,
for it is time to seek the LORD that he may
come and rain righteousness upon you.*

HOSEA 10:12 ESV

So often in the Bible, God's examples of living out our faith are embedded in everyday routines. The work we do shows where we put our trust. In Hosea, the people were more concerned about the size and strength of their army, and God's response was strong: "You have plowed iniquity; you have reaped injustice; you have eaten the fruit of lies" (v. 13 ESV).

Maybe you're putting extra time and energy in your job, a specific achievement or acquisition—things tied to money and status. God wants you to see the potential in the hardpacked, unused ground right in front of you. He wants you to engage in tasks that reflect your belief in His promise of faithfulness and provision. However dry your season is, the rains will come. In the discipline of working that fallow ground, you'll find fulfillment, and you'll experience the fullness of God's love.

98

How do your daily actions reflect the source of your hope and trust?

....
....
....
....

Identify fallow ground in your own life that you need to break up, trusting in God's faithfulness.

....
....
....
....
....

In what ways has God been faithful to you this year?

....
....
....
....

Courage in the Calling

*Now after these things, God tested [the faith
and commitment of] Abraham and said to him,
"Abraham!" And he answered, "Here I am."*

GENESIS 22:1 AMP

There are many times in the Bible when God calls out
to His servant and the response is, "Here I am." It's
easier said than done. In this instance, God was about to
ask something audacious of Abraham: Would he willingly
surrender his greatest treasure, his son, to God?

Maybe it's good that Abraham didn't know this was the
request when he set out on the journey with God that day.
This is the slow roll of God's goodness. He maps out a journey
of small steps that build our faith and commitment until we
reach that penultimate moment when we have an opportunity
to step into a fuller understanding of Him.

Have you heard God's voice calling out to you? What
small step is God asking you to take in faith?

Reflect on moments when your faith and commitment have been tested. How did you experience God's goodness or provision?

Our
Everything

Being Made Whole in God

*May God himself, the God who makes
everything holy and whole, make you
holy and whole, put you together—spirit,
soul, and body—and keep you fit for the
coming of our Master, Jesus Christ.*

1 THESSALONIANS 5:23 MSG

F aith changes how you think, feel, and live in the world. It's difficult, but when you rally your head, heart, and hands in the pursuit of becoming more like God, you will experience wholeness and restoration.

You have explored dozens of ways to be more intentional about how you spend your time and how to grow emotionally and spiritually. There's little doubt that some of the things you explored were incredibly helpful, and others maybe flopped. With persistence, you've seen the rhythm of daily life change in some meaningful ways, bringing you closer to God in the process.

As you continue your walk with God, there won't always be significant changes to implement. Make it your intention to be more like Jesus each day, which helps your light shine a little brighter so others can experience the reality of God and the possibility of being made new.

God Restores

*"Moreover, I will give you a new heart
and put a new spirit within you; and I
will remove the heart of stone from your
flesh and give you a heart of flesh."*

EZEKIEL 36:26 NASB

When God restores you, your heart and spirit are changed. New possibilities emerge. Light shines in the darkness, healing comes, hope abounds.

Restoration is different for each of us. Some of us come to faith like a comet hurtling through the atmosphere—it's a spectacular and memorable event. For others, it's a steady evolution. And all of us will experience periods where restoration seems to be on hold. After all, we can't always be growing.

Remember that God's canvas is expansive, and you are part of His kingdom story. When you can't see restoration and growth in your own life, celebrate what He is doing in the world around you.

How have you experienced restoration over the past year?

....
....
....
....
....
....

How is God making things new in the world around you? Ask God to open your eyes to the new things He has in store for you.

....
....
....
....
....
....
....
....
....

God Creates

"Pay close attention now: I'm creating new heavens and a new earth. All the earlier troubles, chaos, and pain are things of the past, to be forgotten. Look ahead with joy. Anticipate what I'm creating: I'll create Jerusalem as sheer joy, create my people as pure delight."

ISAIAH 65:17–18 MSG

In the expanse of space and the beauty of the land and seas, mountains and valleys, and all living things, we stand in awe of God's creative power.

And yet, in this world, you don't have to go out of your way to find trouble, chaos, or pain. If you can set your focus on what God has done and what He is doing still today, it is easier to rise above the brokenness and take hold of new possibilities.

You are made in the image of your Creator. How will you join with Him in making all things new? Take encouragement not only in the fact that God is making heaven and earth new, but also that He takes delight in *you*, the work of His hands.

God's creation can fill you with awe and wonder. How does this shift your focus to our future hope, God's promise of a new creation?

....
....
....
....
....

How could you join God to "make all things new" and be creative this week?

....
....
....
....
....
....
....
....
....

God Protects

*The LORD is my rock and my fortress and
my deliverer, my God, my rock, in whom I
take refuge, my shield, and the horn of my
salvation, my stronghold and my refuge,
my savior; you save me from violence. I call
upon the LORD, who is worthy to be praised,
and I am saved from my enemies.*

2 SAMUEL 22:2–4 ESV

How would life be different if you lived every moment trusting God to be your protection? So much of life is beyond our control, particularly other people and the choices they make. Inevitably, there will be people and things that work in opposition to you, and there will be times when it feels incredibly personal.

In this passage, David praised God for protecting him from King Saul. David's trust in God as his defender steadily grew through a series of close calls. You can turn to the same God to be your refuge. As the "horn of your salvation," God will be your defense, delivering you from your enemies. He provides you with safety in the chaos of this world.

Describe a time in your life when you experienced God's protection.

....
....
....
....
....
....
....

What worry or anxiety do you need to surrender to God? How might this free you up to live differently this week?

....
....
....
....
....
....
....
....

God Is Just

*He is the Rock, his works are perfect, and
all his ways are just. A faithful God who
does no wrong, upright and just is he.*

DEUTERONOMY 32:4 NIV

If you have more than what you need in this life, injustice might not be a front-of-mind issue as you walk out your faith. And yet throughout the Bible, God is making a way for His people out of slavery, out of oppression, out of suffering.

Injustice has a way of making us feel small and inconsequential; it bullies us into submission. But if we sit back and do nothing, the patterns of this world will continue interrupted. We serve a God who is faithful and just, so as His people, we also need to stand up to injustice.

To embrace what is just, your idea of what is possible might need to change. It's easy to put your head down and mind your own business, but God asks us to see the world as He does.

Is there a particular injustice that weighs on your mind?

....

....

....

....

How could you act or partner with others to address this injustice?

....

....

....

....

Write a prayer that God would open your eyes to new possibilities, giving you a front-row seat to His righteousness and compassion.

....

....

....

....

God Is Good

*Open your mouth and taste, open
your eyes and see—how good GOD is.
Blessed are you who run to him.*

PSALM 34:8 MSG

You are invited to taste and see that God is good. It's human nature to be both curious and doubtful, so God invites you to experience His goodness for yourself. What's more, God's goodness can be found in unexpected places.

As our Heavenly Father, God gives us some clear boundaries on how to live. Accept the invitation to taste and see how even His boundaries might be evidence of His goodness. When you choose to live out your relationships and priorities within these boundaries, you are likely to taste His goodness in new ways. You might come to understand the love behind the boundary in a new light.

Since the beginning of time, God has been showing us that He has good things for us. He both meets our needs and gives us good gifts. And like a good father, God invites you to run to Him when things go wrong.

How have you experienced God's goodness in your life recently?

....

....

....

....

....

 Identify something in your daily life that keeps you from tasting and seeing that God is good. Put some boundaries around that in the week ahead.

....

....

....

....

....

....

....

....

....

God Is Patient

The Lord does not delay [as though He were unable to act] and is not slow about His promise, as some count slowness, but is [extraordinarily] patient toward you.

2 PETER 3:9 AMP

You are a work in progress. This is likely more frustrating for you than it is for God, who abounds in patience. Choosing to follow God is committing to a process of repentance. You will have to root out some stubborn habits along the way. Bad habits often stick because they meet a need, albeit in an unhealthy way. God knows what we need and invites us to embrace a better way of life.

Along your faith journey, you will make corrections and changes—some of them hundreds of times. Don't be discouraged. Be persistent. Trust God to give you what you need and to finish the work He began in you.

How has God shown patience to you?

In what ways are you impatient with yourself as you work to break bad habits and make good ones?

God Is Love

We have come to know [by personal
observation and experience], and have
believed [with deep, consistent faith] the
love which God has for us. God is love, and
the one who abides in love abides in God,
and God abides continually in him.

1 JOHN 4:16 AMP

To abide is to continue without fading or being lost. As you
experience the fullness of God's love, you will see the
limitless nature of it. You are invited to abide in that love.

Humanity often treats love as a commodity, a result of
attractive qualities, ample opportunity, or exceptional talents.
Some think love is something to "find," which keeps us from
feeling alone. Others think it's "earned," which helps us feel
worthy.

God's love came first. You don't need to compete for it,
look high and low for it, or earn it. This realization might take
years to fully understand—that's how radically different God's
love is.

Now contemplate how God is abiding in you and you in
Him. This is how God creates a new heart in you, renews
your mind, and spurs you to action. He moves right into your
everyday life, establishing love as a new rhythm that is felt by
you and others in all that you do.

How has your knowledge and experience of God's love changed over time?

....

....

....

....

....

....

....

Write a verse or a prayer that affirms God's love and repeat it hourly throughout the day. Observe the effect of this on your everyday routine.

....

....

....

....

....

....

....

God Is Faithful

*Understand, therefore, that the LORD your God
is indeed God. He is the faithful God who
keeps his covenant for a thousand generations
and lavishes his unfailing love on those
who love him and obey his commands.*

DEUTERONOMY 7:9 NLT

God is faithful. That is why we don't give up on doing His will, however difficult it can be. Regardless of how many times we've fallen short of obeying His commands, God doesn't give up on us.

How can you be more faithful in response to our faithful God? It takes discipline to deny your human nature and live the way God wants you to live. It's a lifelong practice, regardless of where you are in your faith journey.

God asks us to walk a narrow path, and there is some steep and rigorous ground to cover. Sometimes obedience is a moment-by-moment choice to put one foot in front of the other. We need to make the task smaller and be faithful in each small step, trusting God's unfailing love for what comes next.

How have you seen God's faithfulness in your family (including faith family) from generation to generation?

....

....

....

....

....

....

 Identify some challenges you're facing in this season. What routines or spiritual disciplines would help you remain faithful and obedient?

....

....

....

....

....

....

....

God Is Worthy

*The Spirit of God has made me, and the
breath of the Almighty gives me life.*

JOB 33:4 ESV

It is easy to worship God in good times. It is infinitely more difficult to respond as Job did when loss and tribulation rock your world. Thankfully, God knows your need and supplies the breath in your lungs.

Into the loss, into the chaos, into the personal struggle comes the breath of the almighty God. You are seen. Your pain is fully known. God gives you life. He asks you to trust in His faithfulness, even though the world would look at your circumstances and suggest you walk away.

If you have made it to the other side of one of these trials, you likely credit God for pulling you through. And you are likely changed.

God is worthy of our praise in all circumstances. We call on the same God who answered Abraham, Moses, and David. The same God who sent His son as our Savior, knowing we might need to see God in the flesh, knowing we would want to feel understood. Call out to God and feel His life-giving breath sustaining you.

Describe a time when God breathed hope and life into your struggle.

....

....

....

....

 How did this change your understanding of God?

....

....

....

....

Set aside an hour this week to journal, pray, or walk in nature. What are some of the many ways God is worthy of your praise?

....

....

....

....

....

God Is Steadfast

Oh give thanks to the Lord, for he is good;
for his steadfast love endures forever!

PSALM 118:1 ESV

As you strive to emulate God, you will find it particularly challenging to be steadfast. After all, humans are fickle creatures. But we serve a God who is steadfast in His promises and in His love for us—forever unwavering and unchanging. You will break your habits, make mistakes, and fall short of your goals, yet God will remain the same. He invites you to get back up and try again.

In the effort to establish or break habits, it's easy to get wrapped up in checking all the boxes every single day. Remember, this journey is not about perfection. Recommit your heart and mind to the process with each new day.

Make it an everyday priority to linger in God's steadfast love. Engage in simple routines that align your head and heart with the things God cares about. Be available to act in service to God and others. With repetition, all of this becomes more like breathing . . . perpetual and life-giving, a steadfast faith.

126

In what area of your life have you become more steadfast in the past year?

 Head, heart, hands—is one of these more difficult for you to consistently focus on with God?

As you look ahead, what routines or disciplines do you plan to pursue to further strengthen your faith?

CHANGE HOW YOU LOOK AT YOUR LIFE

ISBN: 978-0-3104-6172-2

THE WEEKLY PURPOSE PROJECT

What lights a fire in your heart? What are you uniquely suited to do? How do you take the talents God gave you to the next level? *The Weekly Purpose Project* is a 52-week guided journal that offers a transformational journey to guide you through discovering how to create a life of purpose and chase your dreams.